9780902888029
AF469115

Great Western Portrait: *1913-1921*

Compiled by
Adrian Vaughan

Oxford Publishing Co · Oxford

© Oxford Publishing Co. and A. Vaughan

First published 1971

SBN 902888 02 1

The author would like to thank Mrs. W.L. Kenning for her unfailing hospitality and encouragement, driver Charles Turner of Oxford R & M Dept. for his help in identifying the locomen, and Jim Russell for his help in preparing the text to this rather unique collection of pictures.

Printed by B. H. Blackwell (Printing) Ltd., Oxford

Published by

Oxford Publishing Co.,
5 Lewis Close,
Risinghurst, Headington,
Oxford.

Introduction

I used to think that if I ever met a leprechaun I should make one request only— to be spirited back in time to 1910, with a bicycle, camera and films inexhaustible. This dream came close to becoming reality when, after the death of my good friend, Bill Kenning, I helped to sort out his collection of 'railwayana'.

I knew that somewhere in the house was a large collection of plate negatives, taken about 60 years earlier and never printed. In the dusty attic, boxes were piled high, containing station shunting instructions, rule books, working timetables, and in fact any sort of 'working' pamphlet dating back to 1910 and coming from several European countries as well as many English railways.

I opened a large trunk and there they were—boxes and boxes of negatives. Four days of excitement followed. Even the boxes were museum pieces, the labels stating '*Imperial dry plates. 1 Doz. Use Pyro soda developer*'. The contents had lain untouched for nearly 60 years and most of the engines photographed I had never seen. Sixteen railway companies were represented in a collection of over a 1000 negatives. Treasure indeed!

What sort of man was the photographer? He was indeed an 'English Gentleman', the product of a vanished society. Honour, to him, was more than just a name; he cared about people and spent much time working for his community. Coming from an upper class background there was a danger of his acquiring a distorted view of life, so his mother encouraged him to go out, meet and talk with the rest of the world. When he was nine years of age, she bought him a camera, suggested that railwaymen were good examples of honest, hardworking folk, and packed him off to the station at Caterham. Thus began his education. He went to Radley College in 1913, and in the following year his mother died. This new burden was carried bravely, for he continued to work hard at school. His text books, especially mathematics, were liberally altered so as to bring the problems about trains travelling from A to B more into line with G.W.R. reality. Pictures of guards vans and their markings abounded.

He spent his spare time in Kennington Junction Box with George Blake. George, a fine looking man and a weaver of improbable tales, took Bill in tow after the death of his mother, having Bill at his home during weekends to give the boy some family life. Bill learned a good deal of humanity, first from his mother and then from his hard working friends.

I met Bill in his later years all because of a camera. No. 4079 *Pendennis Castle* was working a Special on the 'New Line' and I had gone over to Haddenham with a *Marion Tropical Soho* camera to photograph it. In the bright sun, this large mahogany and brass reflex camera with red leather bellows was spotted immediately by Bill, thirsting for the unusual, although he was half a mile down the track at the moment he saw it. The photo was lost, owing to a Brush diesel getting in the way at the last moment, but I had found an unusual friend.

Bill usually drove a 1923 Riley open tourer. He bought it whilst at University, drove it very hard in his undergrad days, which was proved by bills for new back axles, gearboxes and radiators, drove it to his wedding and until he died. It was painted in green—Great Western green from Swindon factory, and lined correctly in orange and black. Brass was plentiful—door handles, lamps, and a large and serpentine horn. Strange to say, Bill did not carry a bucket and twelve detonators on his 'locomotive', as per Rule 127(i) but the following emergency kit *was* carried:— On the outside running board: 1 gallon can 'Pratt's Motor Spirit' and 1 bundle chimney sweeping rods; on the back seat: firewood, large holdall containing Hungarian W.T.T.s and German ditto, hundreds of photographs marked on the back '*Not in common use. Return to W.L. Kenning*', a bicycle, various magpie and crow nests, and miscellaneous trophies picked up en route; in front with him: 1 red, 1 green flag, guard's whistle, notebook and pencil, and working T.T. of journey he was making; on rear of car: Ex L.B.S.C.R. sign 'LV' (in lieu of tail lamp).

When he was coming on a visit to a signal box, a letter of notification was sent enclosing a timetable of the journey. Recovery time was included to offset delays caused by 'Magcrow' operations. Bill's second hobby was bird watching. He was a member of several conservationist societies, but he could not abide magpies or crows because, he said,

'They are cannibals'. If he spotted a crow's nest he assembled his chimney sweeping rods and poked it down and if necessary he would climb the tree with his rods. This was 'operation magcrow'. Having brought down the nest, it was put on the back with the others.

Quite untiring in his pursuit of railways, he roamed this country and the continent with his wife. She was as game as he, braving all weathers in the slow, open Riley. Dawn of April 21st found Bill and Mrs. Kenning peering through the mist hoping to see the sun through the bore of the Box Tunnel. April 21st is the great Brunel's birthday, and the sun is in exactly the right position to shine straight through the tunnel as it rises. Smoke and steam nearly always prevented them from seeing anything through the tunnel, but they always tried!

He was well known at Old Oak Common as 'The Colonel' and spent hours and hours riding the Paddington pilots on the empty stock, doubtless doing his share of the firing. He and his wife made friends with railwaymen all over this country and abroad and Bill kept up a lively correspondence with several of them. These letters were witty and often his reply to a certain point would be no more than a biblical reference. He knew the Old Testament very well, for he always came up with a punning, relevant quote.

His camera was a miracle and with bellows full of holes, and lens not always parallel to film, he got results from subjects anyone else would have called impossible. A sharp blow was needed to open it—a fence or signal post was usually handy, or if not, the rails were always there. When it was brought smartly into contact with a fence post, the lid flew open, and like a Jack in the Box the lens and bellows dangled earthwards. Gathering up the bellows quickly the lens mount was wedged in position on its rails with matchsticks. Bill could take reasonably sharp pictures at even up to 60 seconds exposure, even though he had no tripod, no exposure meter and in fact a very dilapidated camera.

He died from a heart attack high in a Sussex oak while sawing off a branch to improve the view from his kitchen. I am delighted to have known him—an example of all that was best in the English tradition, learned, witty, unostentatious although eccentric, and humane.

November 1971

Adrian Vaughan

1

Departure platform no. 2 at Paddington in 1917, usually for Bristol expresses. The train engine has just backed on, as can be seen by the reversing screw in back gear, and large ejector open. The front guard is just about to give the driver the loading. The engine is in First World War austerity finish, with the safety valve bonnet and copper top to the chimney painted over, etc., with no lining, and all brass beading removed.

No. 4032 *Queen Alexandra* was one of the 'Queen' series built in October 1910 and was fitted with the No. 3 superheaters. Also of note is the 3,500 gallon tender with the long coal side fenders. This batch was the first to be equipped with these enlarged tenders. It was rebuilt as 'Castle' class in April 1926.

2

Departure platform No. 1 at Paddington in 1917, this time with a West of England express. It is interesting to note the layout prior to modernization in the 1930s. The old timber departure box can be seen at the head of platform No. 2. All points and signals were manually operated as can be seen by the levers in the box. Note also the 70ft. coach at the head of the train, reserved no doubt for the use of soldiers on leave, judging from the heads looking out!

Engine No. 4004 *Morning Star* built in 1907 was one of the first batch of 4-6-0 express four cylinder engines, which carried many of the illustrious names borne by the original broad gauge 'Star' class of 1839-41. This locomotive ran forty-one years before being withdrawn in 1948.

A line of three passenger link engines on the ash road at Old Oak Common. These engines are facing East, so have obviously worked into Paddington, backed down from the terminus, and are stood on the ash road either to have their fires cleaned or dropped, before being turned ready for their next link. The first engine is No. 4001 *Dog Star* preceded by a large 'County' tank, and in the lead another 'Star' still retaining its copper topped chimney.

No. 4001 *Dog Star* was the first of the class to have the curved drop to the footplating, which was a great improvement aesthetically on the prototype of the class, *North Star*, which had straight footplating back to the rear of the cab.

4

No. 4016 'Star' class *Knight of the Golden Fleece* backs onto what was probably the Worcester-Hereford position of an express from Paddington, in the middle of the down platform at Oxford. Expresses ran from Paddington to Oxford composed of two parts, the front section for Banbury, Birmingham and Wolverhampton, and the rear position for the Worcester line. The train would halt in Oxford platform so that the Worcester portion was to the rear of the scissors crossover shown. After the front part of the train had departed for the Banbury line, the Worcester train locomotive, which had been standing on the middle road, would back across the scissors, attach, and depart via Yarnton and Honeybourne. No. 4016 was built in 1908 and was one of the batch to carry the improved bogies with side control springs, cribbed from the French de Glehn engines. It was scrapped in 1951 having been rebuilt as a 'Castle' class in 1925.

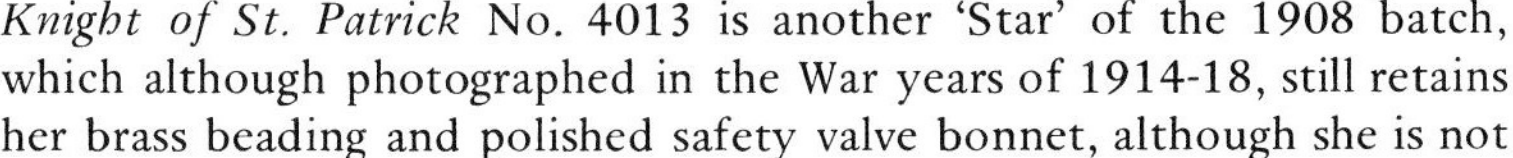

Knight of St. Patrick No. 4013 is another 'Star' of the 1908 batch, which although photographed in the War years of 1914-18, still retains her brass beading and polished safety valve bonnet, although she is not lined out. Notice also the bogie brakes which were fitted at this time, but subsequently removed, as they did not prove very effective. This engine was not scrapped until May 1950.

6

One of the early 'King' series of 'Stars', No. 4023 *King George* shown at possibly the south end of Oxford station on a vacuum freight. Points of interest are the change in the shape of the inside valve covers on the front buffer beam, and few judicious curves, taking away the box like cover fitted before. Note also the superheater header damper, a small steam operated piston, which, when steam was admitted to the cylinder, opened the damper in the smokebox, whilst counterweights closed it when the regulator was shut. This precaution against the burning of superheater bends was found to be unnecessary and was given up with the No. 3 superheater.

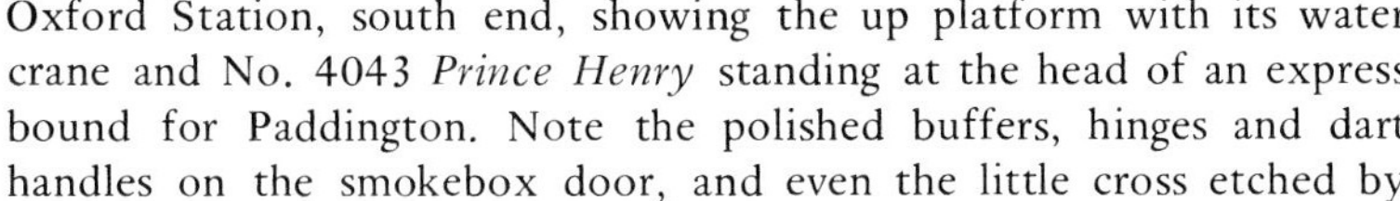

Oxford Station, south end, showing the up platform with its water crane and No. 4043 *Prince Henry* standing at the head of an express bound for Paddington. Note the polished buffers, hinges and dart handles on the smokebox door, and even the little cross etched by emery paper! These details used to be the trademark of Wolverhampton shed. No. 4043 was built in 1913, and finally scrapped in 1952, after nearly forty years of service.

One of the two cylinder 'Saint' class of locomotives, backing onto its train at No. 1 platform, Paddington, prior to departure with a West of England express. Note the coach livery is in the dark lake of the 1916 period, also the large 17 gallon milk churns at the top end of the longest platform. It used to be possible to roll two of these along on their bottom rims, one to each hand but one had to be an expert! The fine gleaming (even if austere) locomotive was one of the 'Saint' class built in March 1913 and of the 'Court' series *Twineham Court* No. 2952 was not withdrawn until September 1951.

A wet day at Radley in 1914 with a rainbow in the sky, as No. 2922 *Saint Gabriel* calls with what is obviously a stopping train. The driver in charge is Jim Griffin, and note the gleaming copper steam pipes by his right hand, only part of his immaculate engine just out from 'shops' I assume. No. 2922 was one of the second series of the 2900 class, the first being the 'Ladies' in 1906, and then the 'Saints' proper in 1907. *Saint Gabriel* ran for 37 years and although only a two cylinder engine, could take its share on all the top link expresses.

The local passenger train on the Thame branch calls at Wheatley in 1921. At the head of the train is a spotless 'Mogul' No. 6386. As this engine was not built until September 1921 she is no doubt just new from Swindon. This would explain the superb condition. Note the long shadows of both the photographer and the starting signal in the 'off' position, also the platform lamps with the paraffin burners. The ladies are all wearing their 'maxis'! A placid scene, but less than twelve months ahead was the general strike when all the railways were paralysed. The reason? Long hours of work and very low wages!

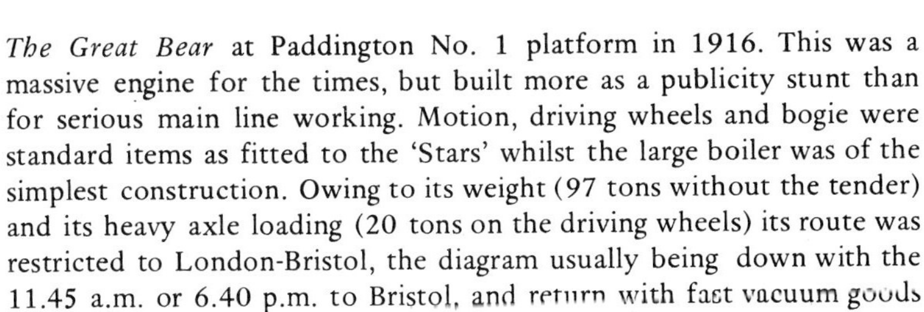

The Great Bear at Paddington No. 1 platform in 1916. This was a massive engine for the times, but built more as a publicity stunt than for serious main line working. Motion, driving wheels and bogie were standard items as fitted to the 'Stars' whilst the large boiler was of the simplest construction. Owing to its weight (97 tons without the tender) and its heavy axle loading (20 tons on the driving wheels) its route was restricted to London-Bristol, the diagram usually being down with the 11.45 a.m. or 6.40 p.m. to Bristol, and return with fast vacuum goods trains. In the early days, enginemen found the locomotive difficult to steam as the extra large firebox (41.7 sq. feet as compared with the 'Stars' 27.7 sq. feet) took a lot of getting used to, but in her latter days, when the experienced man became acclimatized, she steamed well.

Points of interest in this photograph include the extra long smoke box dart handles, the large 15″ cylinders on the engine, and the two arm backing signals just above the shunting engine.

12

The original French compound engine *La France* shown at Didcot yard in the 1917 period. She is seen in the final rebuild stage, with the Swindon superheated No. 1 boiler and fittings. This locomotive was the first and smallest to be purchased by the Great Western Railway in 1903 from the Société Alsacienne des Constructions Méchaniques of Belfort, France, for comparative trials with similar Swindon built 'simple' engines. Although a lot was learned from these engines, like balanced four cylinder layout, slide bars and motion brackets, bogie control and fluted coupling rods, the complication of compounding did not match up to the high pressure simple locomotive.

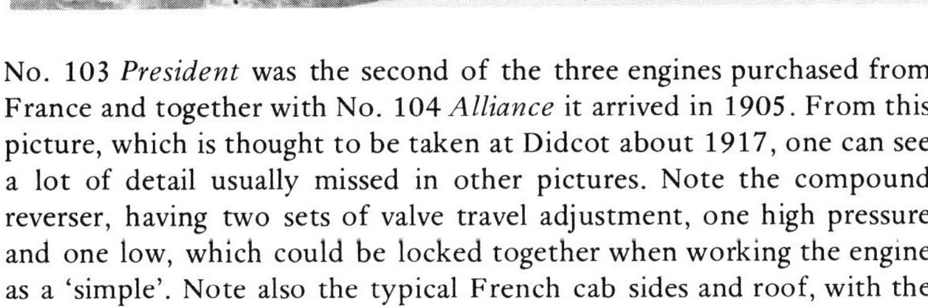

No. 103 *President* was the second of the three engines purchased from France and together with No. 104 *Alliance* it arrived in 1905. From this picture, which is thought to be taken at Didcot about 1917, one can see a lot of detail usually missed in other pictures. Note the compound reverser, having two sets of valve travel adjustment, one high pressure and one low, which could be locked together when working the engine as a 'simple'. Note also the typical French cab sides and roof, with the round topped window, the reducing valve mounted on the smokebox side through which exhaust steam was passed to the low pressure cylinders, and the delicate Welschaerts valve gear which Churchward described as 'watch-makers' work'.

This engine with its two sisters spent the last years of its life shedded at Oxford, and was finally scrapped in 1927.

No. 3700 *Durban* standing in the down platform at Oxford in 1917. The story is told that this engine, which had been shedded at Worcester, was envied by the Oxford foreman, 'Jobber' Brown, who got it transferred to his own shed to the delight of the Worcester locomotive depot, as the engine was a poor steamer. However, this could be conjecture, as the powers that were at Swindon, were hardly likely to be swayed by the likes and dislikes of a humble shed foreman! Nevertheless it is delightful to see this clean looking 'City' class waiting for the 'right-away' at the head of her train. Before the coming of the 'Stars' these engines handled all of the main expresses, replacing the 4-2-2 singles.

No. 3717 *City of Truro* is one of this class and is now preserved at Swindon.

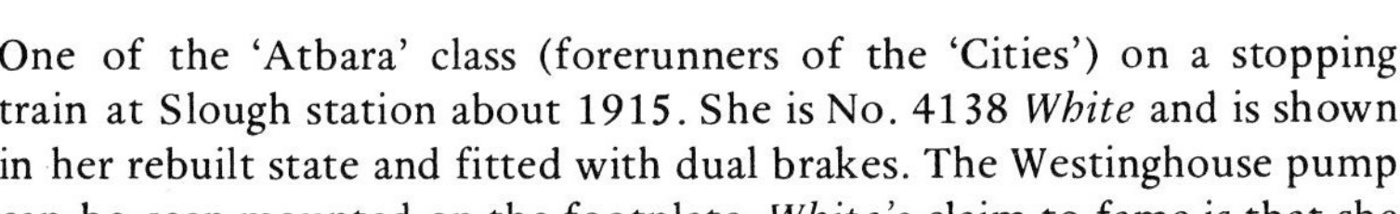

One of the 'Atbara' class (forerunners of the 'Cities') on a stopping train at Slough station about 1915. She is No. 4138 *White* and is shown in her rebuilt state and fitted with dual brakes. The Westinghouse pump can be seen mounted on the footplate. *White's* claim to fame is that she was the only one of her class which, when rebuilt in 1910, did not have the large sandboxes fitted, as seen on *Durban* in the preceding picture. Note also the nameplate on the cab—this oval name and numberplate was only carried by the first 23 engines in the class.

A 'Badminton' rebuild, No. 4102 *Blenheim* starts off from No. 5 platform at Paddington on a stopping passenger train for Oxford about 1915. Note the empty stock train waiting to pull in after the departure of No. 4102. Note also how the starting signals carry their appropriate platform numbers on the face; the shorter arm underneath is a shunt signal to allow movements within station limits.
This particular 'Badminton' class locomotive was built in May 1898 and ran until 1928.

A gleaming 'Bulldog' class No. 3445 *Flamingo* and its crew of Driver Webb and Fireman Williams who pose for Bill Kenning at Oxford in 1915. This picture shows an unusual combination of clean engine and dull tender—one wonders what circumstances caused this. The engine is carrying 'A' headlights, probably waiting to back onto an incoming train. Although of the small 5′8″ driving wheel variety, these 'Bird' class engines did much short distance fast train work, such as Oxford-Paddington, or Oxford to Banbury and Leamington. No. 3445 was built in 1909 and lasted until B.R. days when it was scrapped in 1948.

Slough Middle signalbox, looking towards Paddington in 1916. A train of clerestory coaches, painted in crimson lake, coasts into the down relief road, headed by one of the four 'Armstrong' class 4-4-0's, No. 4169 *Brunel*. She is shown in the final rebuild condition, when her handsome tall chimney and polished dome have been replaced, and her straight boiler changed for the Belpaire firebox and three quarter coned boiler. Even the large 7ft wheels have been reduced to the standard 6'8" drivers, so that she is to all intents and purposes a 'Flower' class. Built in 1894, she ran until 1928.

An interesting photograph of the 1917 period, taken at Paddington, probably from the end of the long No. 1 or 'A' platform, which was an attractive vantage point for enthusiasts and photographers alike in those days. It shows a 'Bulldog' class, No. 3413 *James Mason*, pulling back a local passenger train, after it has been emptied on the arrival side. Note the backing signal at the left with its six way route indicator, also the fogman's hut and upturned fire devil nearby.

'Bulldog' class No. 3452 *Penguin* in wartime austerity finish standing in the down platform at Oxford. Judging from the 'B' headcode, she is on a local stopping passenger train, probably to Banbury or Worcester. The picture would have been taken in winter time as one can see the steam heating leaking slightly between the tender and the first coach. Notice also the low roofed passenger stock in the bay, which was usually kept for trains to the Fairford branch.

On a murky day in 1914, No. 3027 *Worcester* leaves Paddington with the 11.15 a.m. for Worcester. The engine is seen in her final form, just before scrapping in July 1914. When first built in 1891, she was named *Thames* but subsequently altered to *Worcester* in December 1895, rather an appropriate name as for many of her later years she was shedded at Worcester. It will be seen from this lovely action picture that, although the big brass dome has been painted over, the engine still retains her copper capped chimney and polished brass safety valve bonnet.

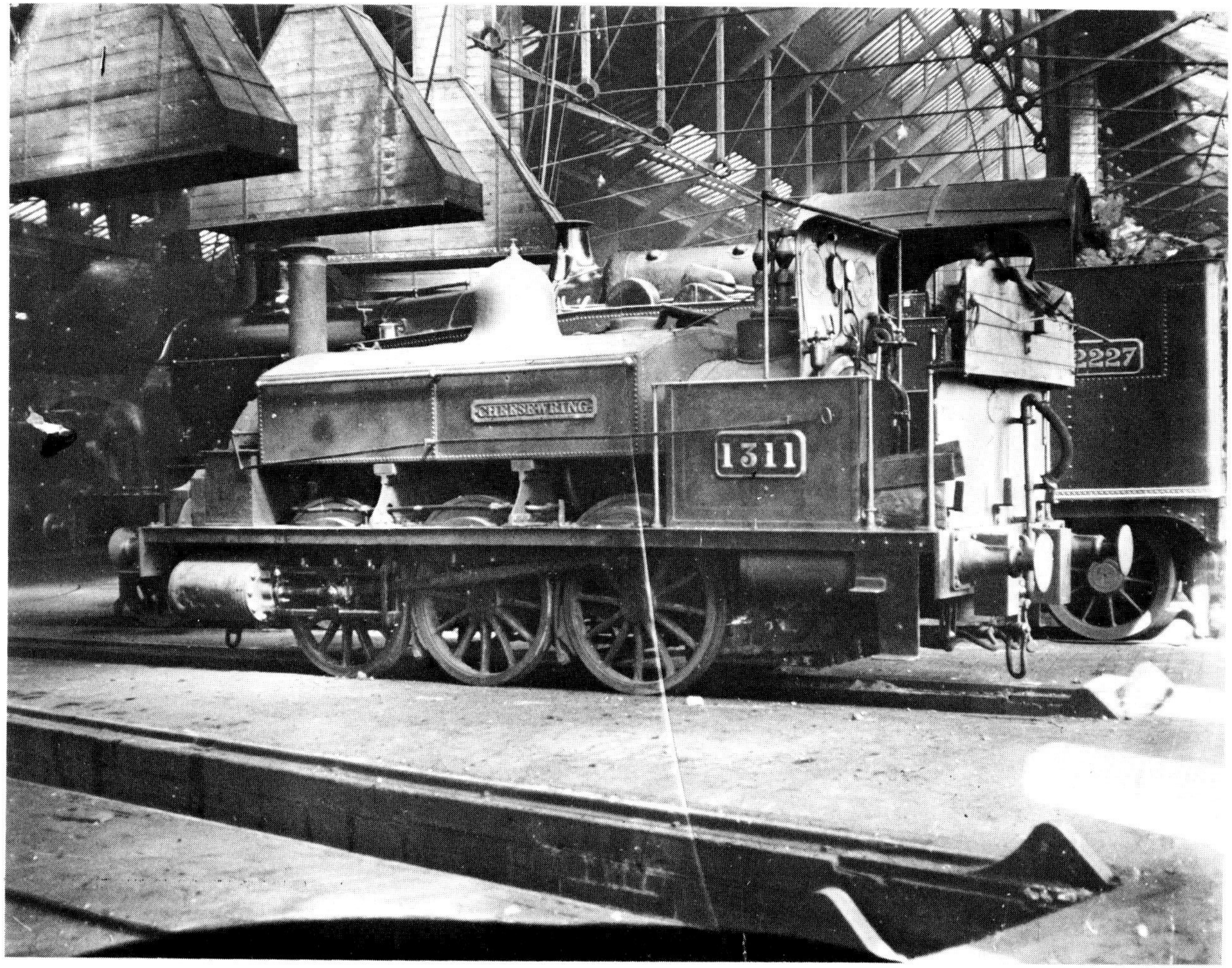

Inside Old Oak Common Shed in 1917. A large 'County' tank No. 2227 towers over the little 0-6-0 saddle tank *Cheesewring*, one of the engines absorbed into the Great Western stock in 1909 from the Liskeard and Looe Railway. This particular engine, No. 1311, was built by Gilkes, Wilson & Co. and was one of their long boiler type of saddle tanks. She dates from 1864, and so had 45 years on the clock before being 'adopted' by the G.W.R. and finishing her days pottering about at Old Oak Common of all places. Notice the primitive weatherboard protection for the enginemen, the non standard controls, and the long lever to the sandbox along the water tank! She was finally withdrawn in 1919.

No. 2655 ‘Aberdare’ class on a down freight near the 59 mile post on the Oxford line. These engines were the freight versions of the ‘Bulldogs’ and ‘Atbaras’ but with the 2-6-0 wheel arrangements instead of the 4-4-0. The engine is shown in the pre-1914 condition with the special shaped chimney, copper capped, and the polished safety valve bonnet. Notice the polished buffer heads and smokebox door hinges etc. One thing of interest is the headcode. I learn from old drivers that this positioning indicated ‘D’ code ‘Through goods to destination’. The nearest other to this was three across as shown, and one on the chimney, but this was for Royal trains only.

Another picture of the eastern end of Slough station, showing one of the early 2-6-0 'Moguls' running quietly through on the down relief road. This is No. 4329 built in 1913, and was one of the first to be nine inches longer than the first twenty engines. These mixed traffic engines were very versatile, and could handle any traffic from slow goods to cross country expresses. Although their driving wheels were only 5′8″ diameter, they could run quite fast, and the story is told in later years of a freight train headed by a 53xx overtaking the *Cheltenham Flyer* when Mr. Collett was a passenger. At the time he was considering the design of the 'King' class, and this incident is said to have decided the point of smaller driving wheels for them! Note here that this train also has the three headlamp code!

This photograph was taken at Oxford some time in the First World War period, and shows one of the 31xx class of 2-6-2T standing on the middle road at the south end of Oxford Station. These engines were the forerunners of the mixed traffic 'Moguls' and preceded them by six years. Mr. Churchward built the prototype of the class, No. 99, in 1903 and tried out the design thoroughly for two years before going ahead and ordering eighty over the next five years. They numbered from 3100 (old 99!), 3111-49 and 3150-3190 with larger boilers. Note in this picture the step in the footplating before the advent of graceful curves, and also the painted over boiler fittings, indicative of the war years. Also in the picture can be seen the inspection pit on the up platform road.

One of the 'Birdcage' 2-4-2T locomotives standing at Slough station in 1914. Most of these locomotives were allocated to suburban trains in the Birmingham and London areas, and this No. 3611 is no doubt on a slow passenger train, working up to Paddington. Points of interest are the large round spectacle glass brass bound, the square coal bunker, volute springs to the pony wheels, and the large air vents in the side tanks made necessary as these engines carried water pick-up scoops. On the first engine in the class (then numbered No. 11), when picking up water at speed, the small vents originally were insufficient to get rid of the air, and so pressure built up and split the tanks horizontally.

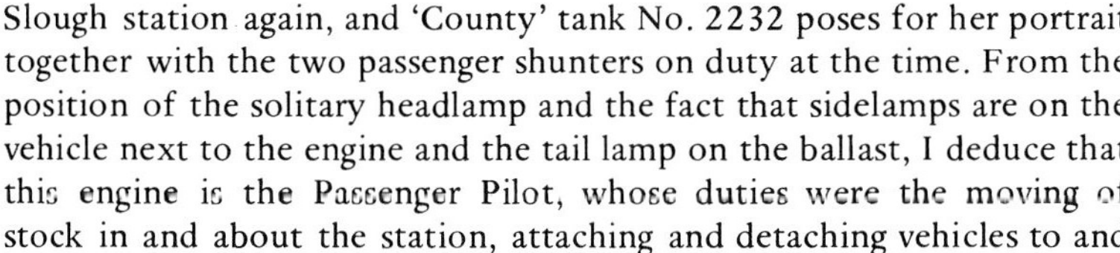

Slough station again, and 'County' tank No. 2232 poses for her portrait together with the two passenger shunters on duty at the time. From the position of the solitary headlamp and the fact that sidelamps are on the vehicle next to the engine and the tail lamp on the ballast, I deduce that this engine is the Passenger Pilot, whose duties were the moving of stock in and about the station, attaching and detaching vehicles to and from trains etc. Many of the larger stations kept these pilots in steam for the 24 hours as, should any main line engine have a failure, these pilots could immediately deputise. What large high standing engines these were! Note the ducting on top of the water tanks, which was part of the two-way water pick-up scoop, as on the '36xx' class.

One of the 'County' class proper, No. 3833 *County of Dorset*, is seen standing on the bridge over the Duke's Cut at Oxford, North. As the reversing lever is shown in back gear and she is on the up middle road, I assume that she is waiting to back across the road on to the shed. One of the backing signals and Oxford Station North box can just be seen above the tender top. These engines were fitted with the same size wheels, motion and cylinders etc. as the previous '22xx' class, which is why the latter were always known as the 'County' tanks.

A picture which disproves the theory that all engines of this period were spotlessly clean. Here at Slough on the way up to Paddington, Mr. Kenning catches the prototype 'County', No. 3800 *County of Middlesex*, as she starts off with all the signals 'off' for the last lap to London. The position of the regulator shows that she is not just flying through, and the fact that she has a loco inspector on the footplate indicates that perhaps all is not quite well. These engines, having a high centre of gravity, with just four 6′8½″ drivers and short wheelbase, were very unstable engines and required a lot of maintaining to keep in top link order. In their day they were known as 'Churchward's rough riders'.

30

The down bay at Oxford in the 1917 period, and the occupant is No. 73 *Isis*, an engine with a really long history. The class, known as the 'Rivers', were seven strong and started life in 1855-6. They were the first standard gauge passenger engines to be built for the G.W.R. by Beyer Peacock & Co. Originally they were of the 2-2-2 wheel classification but, as they were so light and loads got heavier, they were sent to Swindon in 1895 where they were reconstructed as 2-4-0's. The old frames were retained but lengthened, and if one looks at the photograph it is possible to see the join where the new arched framing and footplating was fitted. Note also the early tender which has been 'modernised' by fitted coal plates in place of the rails.

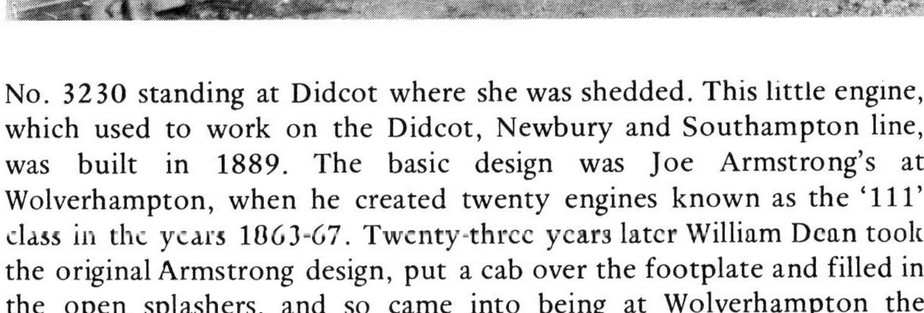

No. 3230 standing at Didcot where she was shedded. This little engine, which used to work on the Didcot, Newbury and Southampton line, was built in 1889. The basic design was Joe Armstrong's at Wolverhampton, when he created twenty engines known as the '111' class in the years 1863-67. Twenty-three years later William Dean took the original Armstrong design, put a cab over the footplate and filled in the open splashers, and so came into being at Wolverhampton the '3226' class. There were only six engines in the class, and bore the doubtful distinction of being the last tender engines to be built at Wolverhampton. The tender of 3230 is also of interest as it was originally made specially by Dean for the 'Duke' class in 1895. Its small size was necessary because in the West Country the existing turntables were not long enough to take engines fitted with larger tenders. Note the tall 'home' signal on Didcot east curve.

This plate portrays No. 2220 standing in an Oxford area station at the head of a parcels train, which is indicated by the old type headcoding. This engine was the last of her '2001' class to be built and was turned out of Swindon shops in October 1882, ran some 1,200,000 miles, and finally met her end in September 1921. Originally she had the long domeless boiler, type S.0. which was changed to the S.4 type in 1898, and finally given the B4 type in September 1916, as shown in the photograph. Three points of interest are worthy of note: 1. The number plate is not only fixed to the rear splasher but also on a separate plate of its own. 2. The two separate brass beadings to each driving wheel splasher. 3. The old sandwich type of tender, similar to that attached to *Isis* on page 30.

The fancy roof of the station buildings in this picture identify it as Slough again, and the date about 1914. The locomotive shown is the final development of the previous '2210' class described, namely the '3232's'. These engines resembled the '22xx's' very closely, but had one or two distinguishing features such as the numbers were mounted on the splasher individually and not contained in a plate. Also the brass beading was in a continuous strip and not divided as before. No. 3236 was built in 1892, had four boiler changes in her 34 years of life, and ran about 1,000,000 miles in that time. It is on record that one of these engines, No. 3240 working the Night Mail from Shrewsbury to Bristol, attained 93 m.p.h. near Hereford in an effort to make up lost time. It must have been quite an experience on the small footplate!

Another 2-4-0 is depicted here but is very different to the '3232's'. This is a 'Barnum' class standing at Radley station about 1916. These locomotives were the most successful and well known of the 'Dean' 2-4-0's. They were the last type with sandwich frames designed and built by the Great Western and when new had Allen-Richardson balanced slide valves underneath the cylinders. When built, all the springs were underhung, but between 1894-7 the springs on the leading wheels were moved on top of the platforms. At the time this picture was taken, No. 3217 was shedded at Oxford and before being cut up in 1935 she ran a remarkable distance of 1,500,000 miles. Notice the hot pipe (for damping the coal and keeping the footplate clean) hanging from the cab handrail.

Another 'Barnum', again at Slough Station, during the First World War years. She is the sister engine to No. 3217 on page 34, but in rather different guise. No. 3218 has the domeless boiler fitted, with safety valve and top feed on the back ring. In this picture she is obviously doing her duty as station pilot, and has probably just taken water at the adjoining water column. Note the side lamp on the four wheel suburban stock standing in the platform just in front of the engine. Also of interest is the gas supply hose which was connected to an underground tank, acting as a reservoir for gassing coaches by the Carriage and Wagon Department. Only large stations had these subterranean reservoirs, other depots using the gas tank vehicles.

One of the railway servants, a platform inspector, obviously a man of integrity and not frightened of hard work. It took years of service to rise to these dizzy heights, but it was open to all employees as long as they lived long enough, did not drink or smoke on duty, and had at least eight hours sleep. So said the rule book of that time! Notice the high stiff collar and frock coat and the gold braid on his cap which was a mark of authority. One other point not generally known is that neckties of this period were red so that they could be used in an emergency to stop a train!

The interior of a typical Great Western signalbox, which is probably Radley. My assumption is that the Guard is in charge of the Abingdon branch train and has come to the box for the single line staff. Note the early type of telephone instruments, and particularly the heavy screening around the oil lamp bracket, which was a war time blackout precaution because of Zeppelins!

Little changed in the boxes for fifty years, the same block instruments being in use till the final demolition. Note that the first four levers from the left are painted white, which indicates that they are spares and the two levers which are pulled would be facing point locks and would be painted blue.

Radley station pictured in the 1914-18 war period. This delightful little station, typically Great Western, was situated between Oxford and Didcot, 59½ miles from Paddington, and was the junction for the Abingdon branch. The view shown is looking north towards Oxford with the two main lines running through the platforms, and the branch loop can be seen on the left hand side of the picture. This branch left the station to the right of the picture and ran alongside the main line for nearly a mile before branching away west to Abingdon. This was just before the main lines crossed over the Thames by Nuneham viaduct. Some points worth noticing are the oil lamp glasses which have been partially blacked out, the general spick and span look of the whole layout and the steel oil drum on the up platform right hand side. These were the standard Swindon 50 gallon drums which were delivered by the stopping goods to every station, containing paraffin oil for the station and signal lamps.

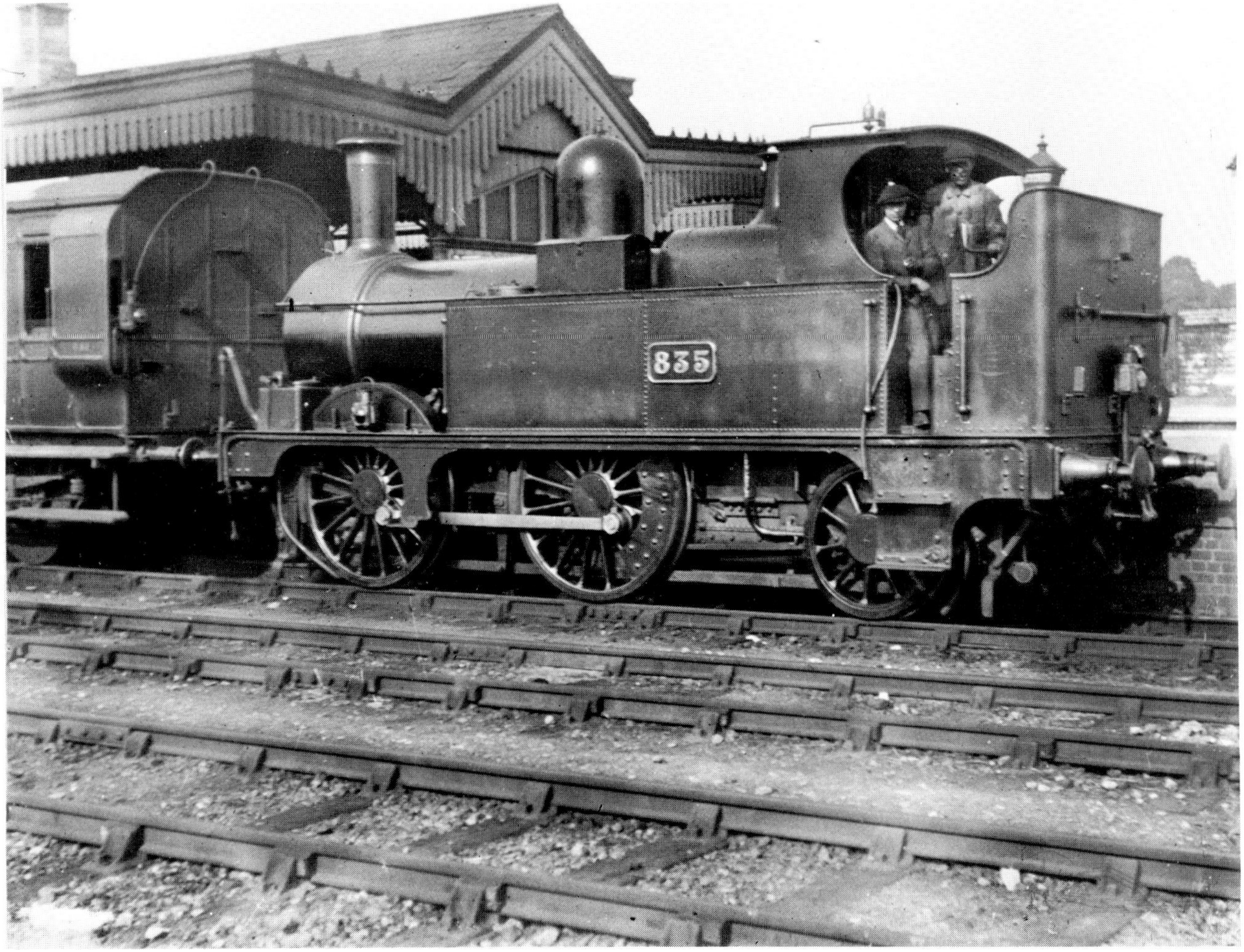

The scene is again Radley Station in the same period as the previous plate. No. 835 is shown standing on her train after having just run round, prior to another departure for Abingdon. This can be assumed as the side lamps are still in place on the four wheel brake third next to the engine. No. 835 is one of the '517' class of 0-4-2 tanks built at Wolverhampton. Her date of construction is given as December 1873, and she survived with many changes until 1935, although records show that she was one of the few which did not receive lengthened frames in the 1890s, which gave more room on the footplates.

Another arrival at Radley. No. 835 in charge of the little train from Abingdon has just reached her journey's end after the 2½ miles trip along the branch. She will now uncouple and run round her coaches via the middle line (shown on page 38). By doing this, no delay was caused to traffic on the main line. Notice the typical Great Western overbridge with its ornate covering, ironwork, and double flights of steps.

The sister engine to No. 835 doing some shunting in the yard at Radley. Both 835 and 522 were shedded at Oxford, and both belonged to the '517' class. However, No. 522 was a much earlier engine than her sister, having been built at Wolverhampton in 1868 with saddle tanks, a bell mouthed chimney and only a bent spectacle plate as protection for the crew. She was converted to side tanks at Swindon in 1894, but retained her short framing as did No. 835. One other subtle difference between the two locos was that No. 522 kept her wooden buffer beam at the front, which made her slightly longer than her sister.

Yet another '517' class engine, No. 1473 *Fair Rosamund*, is shown standing in the bay at Kidlington about 1921. Kidlington was the junction station, situated on the Oxford-Banbury line, where the small branch diverted to Woodstock. No. 1473 is the only example, as far as we know, of a '517' tank engine to bear a name. This name was given on the occasion of a Royal visit to Blenheim Palace in 1896. The original fair Rosamund being a mistress of Henry II, this appears to have been a somewhat doubtful gesture to Queen Victoria, but it seemed to pass unnoticed, as 1473 carried her name until being scrapped in 1938. It is very nice to see in the picture stationmaster Cook in his black overcoat and pillbox hat with the gold leaf. In those days station masters were rated in the village to have the same social status as the doctor and vicar!

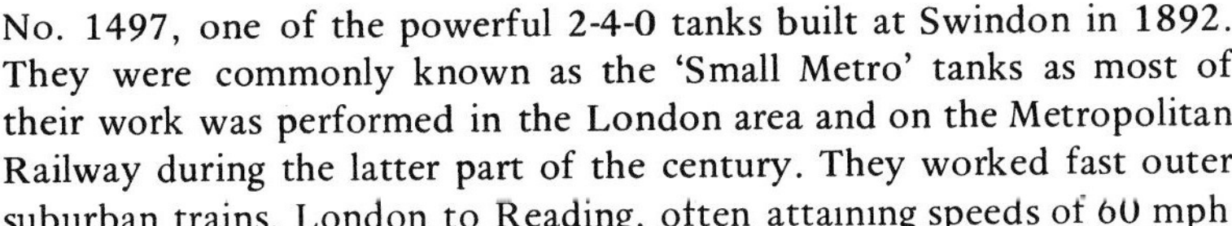

No. 1497, one of the powerful 2-4-0 tanks built at Swindon in 1892. They were commonly known as the 'Small Metro' tanks as most of their work was performed in the London area and on the Metropolitan Railway during the latter part of the century. They worked fast outer suburban trains, London to Reading, often attaining speeds of 60 mph and upwards. The example shown is seen at Oxford about 1917 and points of interest are the large sandbox and mudguard on the engine, the bracket signal with distant arm painted red, and the pre-grouping wagons in the background.

A wet day at Slough, and the head shunter and his mate pose with No. 3584 whilst shunting the sidings of Windsor Works. This engine is one of the Large Metro tanks class, known to enginemen as the 'Dancers'. They were of the same general dimensions as previous engines in the class, but those built in 1899 and after had longer tanks of 1100 gallons capacity. To accommodate these tanks, the sandboxes were placed underneath the platforms, and volute springs were used instead of the laminated, which took up more room. It is said that when running fast they indulged in a sort of dancing motion, frightening to behold, hence their nickname. It is interesting to see in this picture the early type of ground signal, just a straight box painted red, and two spectacles.

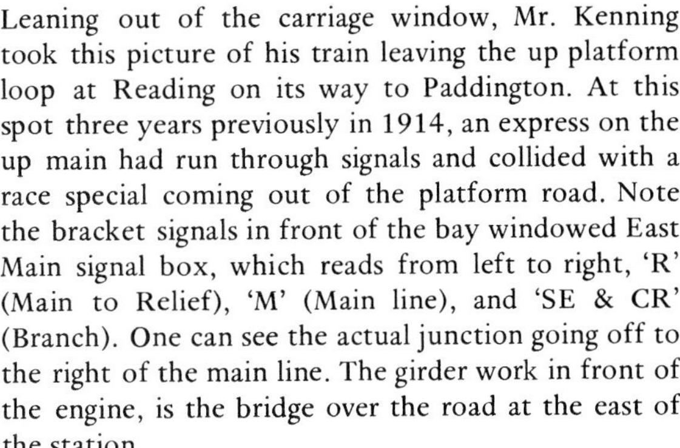

Leaning out of the carriage window, Mr. Kenning took this picture of his train leaving the up platform loop at Reading on its way to Paddington. At this spot three years previously in 1914, an express on the up main had run through signals and collided with a race special coming out of the platform road. Note the bracket signals in front of the bay windowed East Main signal box, which reads from left to right, 'R' (Main to Relief), 'M' (Main line), and 'SE & CR' (Branch). One can see the actual junction going off to the right of the main line. The girder work in front of the engine, is the bridge over the road at the east of the station.

Driver Wilkins of Didcot and his fireman awaiting instructions on the footplate of either a 'City', 'Atbara' or 'Aberdare' class or perhaps even a 'Bulldog'. The fitting of the steam reversing gear does pin-point it down to one of these classes. It is possible to see the cut-off indicator just to the right of and below the vacuum brake handle (the fitting with the holes). Notice the driver's oil feeder in the corner of the cab, and that the engine has the needle of the steam gauge on the red maximum mark, vacuum is shown to be well up, and the other small steam gauge above the fireman's left shoulder shows about 80 lbs. As this was for the steam heating of carriages, I deduce it is winter time and the engine is attached to a passenger train, possibly at Radley again.

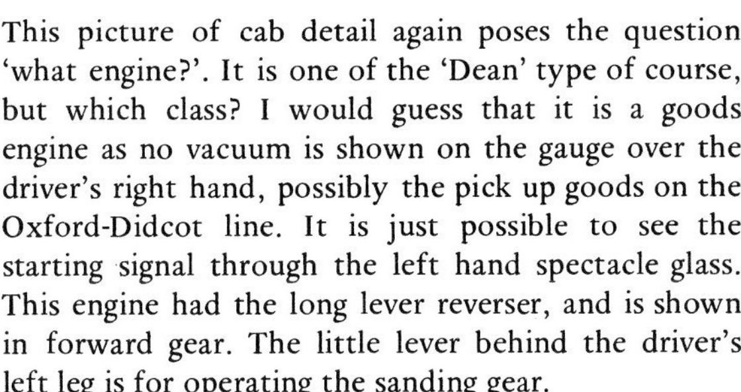

This picture of cab detail again poses the question 'what engine?'. It is one of the 'Dean' type of course, but which class? I would guess that it is a goods engine as no vacuum is shown on the gauge over the driver's right hand, possibly the pick up goods on the Oxford-Didcot line. It is just possible to see the starting signal through the left hand spectacle glass. This engine had the long lever reverser, and is shown in forward gear. The little lever behind the driver's left leg is for operating the sanding gear.

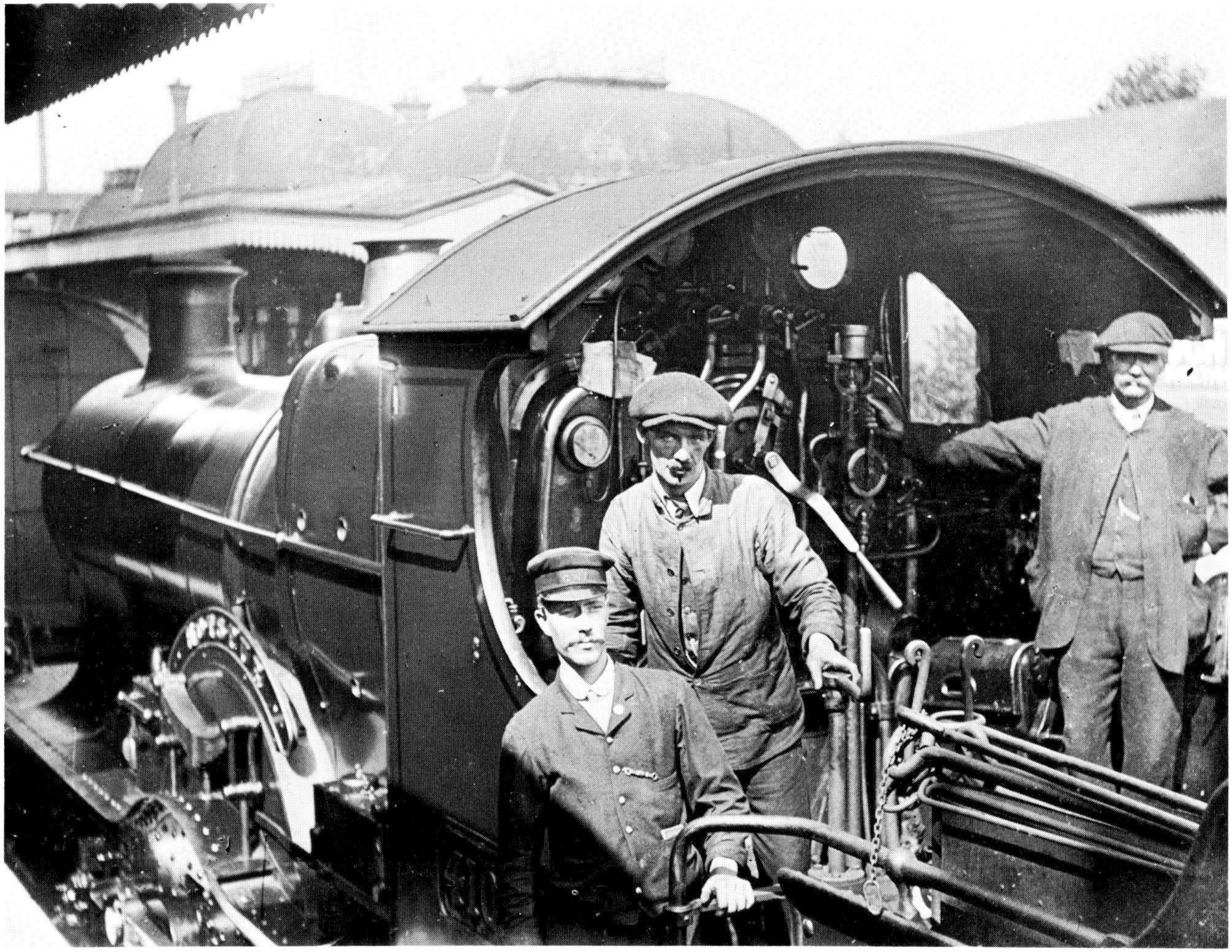

A rebuilt 'Badminton' class in spotless condition is shown doing station pilot duties at Slough. Driver Albert Covey and fireman Ted Burden await instructions from the passenger shunter seen on the steps of the 4-4-0. She is in lovely condition, probably just out of shops after being fitted with piston valves in 1915. Note the screw reversing gear by the side of the driver's right leg, and the spotless running plate bottom left.

A small engine with a chequered history stands on an 'A' headlight express in Slough station during the war years. She is No. 3544 and one of a series of nineteen engines built as broad gauge convertibles 0-4-2 saddle tanks in 1889, converted to 0-4-4 side tanks in 1890-91 and to standard gauge in late 1891. When built in this style they had a reputation for bad running and at speed, riding on the footplate was like 'a dog shaking a rat'. In fact two of the class, Nos. 3521 and 3548, were involved in a derailment at Bodmin Road in 1895. The engine came down the hill fast, flanges smashing sideways at the rails; the track was damaged, though the train passed safely. Following was an express from London, hauled by 3251. As rough riding as ever, it destroyed the few remaining chairs holding the rails, resulting in a serious accident killing several people. Again in 1898 the Falmouth mail train hauled by 3542 at Penryn was derailed and its driver was killed. After this the class was altered to a 4-4-0 tender engine and worked on in this style until the late twenties.

Dean Goods, '2310' class

Designed in 1883, 260 were built in six years. Unrivalled for their combination of robust simplicity and power with light axle loading, they might have been designed with war service in mind. Sixty-two were sent to France in 1917 and only seven were lost and they were part of a group of eighteen sent to Salonika. The 'Salonika' engines returned home two years after the 'French' engines in 1921 and quietly went back to work. Twenty-two years later, 110 were called to war, some for the second time. Of one hundred and ten, nine were taken from the scrap yard and of these seven returned and were later scrapped, but two carried on until 1954. The two that did not come back failed to do so for the very good reason that they were in East Germany and China respectively. Other countries' railways favoured by the presence of the Deans Goods included Egypt, Libya, Turkey and Italy.

On the home front, some were employed in hauling rail mounted coastal defence guns which when fully equipped weighed 800 tons.

Fifty-four survived to become B.R. Class '2MT'. They were to be replaced by a B.R. 'Standard' design based on L.M.S. 2-6-0 46419, of 1948 vintage. When this loco arrived at Swindon for trials, it made a lot of noise on heavy trains, but not much steam. Drivers said that a Dean Goods would be more effective. Comparative trials were held, with very embarrassing results for B.R. Derby. The Dean engine No. 2579 was investigated (not for hidden turbines) and Derby retired for consultation. The result was the improved 46419 as a standard 78xx. The improved but still inferior engine then replaced the remaining Great Western engines.

Two trains awaiting the road into Reading? The line is obviously the S.E. & C. Railway branch from Reading to Ash, and both trains are heading north. (Note the afternoon shadows from the right.) I would assume that the Dean arrived first, could not get a path into Reading and was shunted over on to the wrong road to allow the South Eastern train to come up on the right road. One can see the two engine crews conversing, so they were obviously stationary.

A 'Dean' goods on foreign metals. The location is unknown but perhaps it may even be on the L.B.S.C. Railway at Horsham or Guildford. I think that it may be a train of steam coal for the Royal Navy at Dover, Portsmouth or Newhaven. Notice the interesting point-work and ground signals.

A copper topped chimney adorns this 0-6-0 'Dean' as she manouvres her train of suburban four wheelers into the up relief at Slough. It is again during the years of World War 1 and I would assume from the driver's sun hat that it is summer time. Notice particularly the splendid enamel advertisement signs on the boundary fence. This engine is one of the odd forty, out of a total complement of 380, to be fitted with top feed to the boiler. The suburban set of four wheelers looks distinctly grubby, even allowing for wartime austerity.

No. 2580 'Dean' standard goods engine, carrying 'F' headlights, coasts through Slough on the up relief in 1916. Twelve months later this engine was one of sixty-two which were taken over by the Royal Ordnance Dept. and shipped to France. She returned to this country in 1921, went to work again on the G.W.R., and was called to the colours again in November 1939. The War Department renumbered her No. 111. Like others in war service, she was fitted with Westinghouse brake gear, painted black all over, and the numbers were in large numerals painted on the tender. After the 1939-45 war, she returned to this country and was cut up for scrap. These engines experienced some trouble with the steam brake, which was operated by two cylinders situated under the cab steps. The piston was directly linked to the brake rods and would often jam in the 'on' position, necessitating a couple of heavy blows with the coal pick to release it. Note also in the picture the lime washed cattle truck (Mex) with the number, size and lettering on the end of the vehicle.

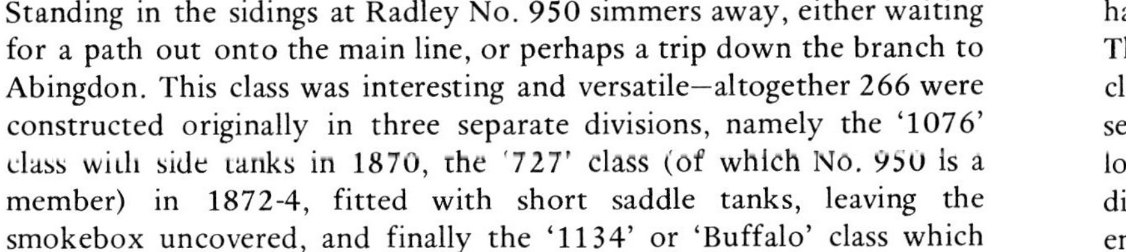

Standing in the sidings at Radley No. 950 simmers away, either waiting for a path out onto the main line, or perhaps a trip down the branch to Abingdon. This class was interesting and versatile—altogether 266 were constructed originally in three separate divisions, namely the '1076' class with side tanks in 1870, the '727' class (of which No. 950 is a member) in 1872-4, fitted with short saddle tanks, leaving the smokebox uncovered, and finally the '1134' or 'Buffalo' class which had full length saddle tanks and were built between 1874 and 1881. They were gradually rebuilt and standardised to form the one '1076' class (with the exception of twelve) and fitted with the pannier tanks as seen in the plate. What is not generally known is that they used to haul long coal freights from South Wales to Swindon and Salisbury for distances of 100 miles and more. Many were the difficulties encountered by shortages of both water and coal!

Another mystery photograph. It is obviously a Great Western single line branch, amongst rolling country with the milepost showing 9½ miles. The Saddle tank, a '27xx' class is seen on the branch goods just entering the passing loop. My guess would be that it is Tiddington on the Thame branch around 1916. The photograph may have been taken from an overbridge.

A fine historical photograph, not only of No. 54, one of the steam railcars, but also of the little platform halt of Abingdon Road, which passed into oblivion in 1921. The site is where a modern by-pass now passes over the road to Oxford just outside Hinksey. Notice that the railcar is painted in the crimson lake livery, and one can just see the engine number, which was always to be found on a brass plate affixed to the engine bogie stretcher. This car was en route from Oxford to Princes Risborough via the Thame branch as this was one of their allocated duties. No. 54 was built new in 1905 and finally withdrawn in 1926.

Another early 'Star' class, standing in the up platform road at Oxford in 1917. She is probably at the head of a slow passenger train to Paddington as she carries the 'B' headcode. Although in the wartime austerity livery, with bright work painted over, it is obvious that much fond attention has been lavished on her. Note the patterns made with oily waste on the rims of the bogie wheels. Also of interest is the fitting of the large ejector along the boiler length under the handrail, and the removal of the superheater damper, which has left a patch on the smokebox. No. 4010 *Western Star* was the last of the first batch of the '40xx' class named after the old broad gauge engines, and was built originally with a Cole superheater for experimental purposes. In 1909 this apparatus was replaced by the standard Swindon type. I would explain here, that where these big 4-6-0's are shown on stopping passenger duties, this would no doubt be as a running-in trip to which all engines straight out from shops were subjected, in the same way in which we run-in a new car.

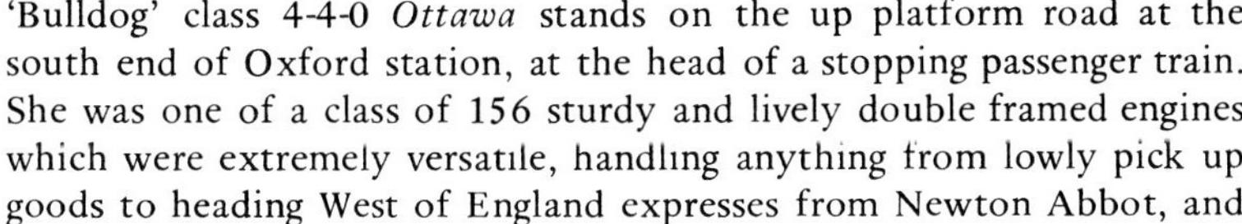

'Bulldog' class 4-4-0 *Ottawa* stands on the up platform road at the south end of Oxford station, at the head of a stopping passenger train. She was one of a class of 156 sturdy and lively double framed engines which were extremely versatile, handling anything from lowly pick up goods to heading West of England expresses from Newton Abbot, and even the *Riviera* itself between 1899 and 1909. No. 3399 herself was built in 1904 and spent 43 years at various depots on all kinds of jobs. It was very odd to see them in their later years piloting massive 'King' class locomotives up the heavy banks west of Newton Abbot.